Under a Pink Sunrise

Karen Kelley

Under a Pink Sunrise

When that sun arrived so early,
the sky was in a dream.
Stars were spinning tenderly.
The Milky Way swirled cream.

As it rounded its longitude,
expressing waking, joy stretches,
and filling the bowl above with pink,
wisps of blue about the edges.

Looking from my tiny point
at the vast beauty of promise,
I declare to give as much today,
and pray God keeps me honest.

Charleston, SC
www.PalmettoPublishing.com

Under a Pink Sunrise
Copyright © 2021 by Karen Kelley

First Edition

Hardcover ISBN: 978-1-63837-294-3
Paperback ISBN: 978-1-63837-295-0
eBook ISBN: 978-1-63837-296-7

I dedicate this work to my maternal grandmother,
Jane Ruth, my namesake.
Though she was strict, all I remember was feeling valued,
and her love.

As this memory of her percolates in my mind overnight,
I realize I have a crowd of loving faces belonging to living
saints, encouraging me all my life.

I could never name them all, but I will try to name a few:

~ T. June, Herbert, Mr. Etan, Charlie, Mary, DeAnna,
Peter A., Ed M., M. Anna, Paul R., and Win-Win ~

Table of Contents

Karen Kelley lives in a rural town in mid-coast Maine where her writing is influenced by New England scenic views. She has been an artist and writer her whole life, writing poetry and exploring many mediums of art. Her love of biology and study of herbology are revealed by simple prose that are exciting, unexpected, lively, colorful, and bursts with nature. When considering relevance on any and all subjects, in her life, there is no other more important detail than Jesus, and the sustaining, abiding Orthodox faith.

She currently is the Lead Administrator of her You Tube channel, Rainbows in the Water.

And Rainbows in the Water.com

Jesus, born of human flesh
to shatter what bound man to earth.
He accepted total humility.
He did not fear their sin or the dirt.

Absolute truth, even if completely destroyed,
was already made record and scored.
No hole, or strike, or earthly fire
in that library, could ever endure.

Earth, but a test for us.
Though primary image, only mental.
And Jesus demonstrated the next paradigm.
The former now becomes provincial.

All relevance became deepened.
Not in dirt, but by your trust He collected.
It plays in tune when seeking holy,
His bowing hand, holy harp, all affected.

He claimed He was telling the truth.
My life is a clear demonstration,
everything He claimed was true.
I seek my heavenly reservation.

His arm, He willingly extended.
His wrist, secured by number 8.
His feet, held by one nail,
suffering to stand straight.

Yes, He did this for me.
He gave all ambition to God.
What He could gain from this rock
was never about being boss.

They did not force His gift.
His life, only taken to the Father.
A cause above sight or understanding
as revelation unfolds without fodder.

Books, notes, prayerful thought,
remembered words of this Man.
Description of His placement;
a Bible was God's plan.

This precious love letter held
His tender effort, never militant.
His life was given for you and I.
His presence within my heart, brilliant.

I asked a lot from God.
I was new at holy thinking.
Misunderstanding forgiveness,
I had no idea, I'd been sinking.

Struggling to control what not.
So strong because I know God.
Busy thinking, pontificating,
still demonstrating sod.

But He shined, and let rain,
and He listened attentive
to my complaints, miles of requests.
My part of our relation, pendentive.

He does not react, our good shepherd.
Training the contemporary herd takes time.
Prayers reflect the hearted song,
demonstrate what is truly divine.

Thoughts on hoped for notions
become lighter by intention,
if eschewing selfish desire.
Less of self for prayerful mention.

God knows the needs to
bring each child home, saved.
As learning ages by reaching,
humility lights the way.

The voice I heard was distinct.
It said only by trust would I hear.
My mind, shocked from sleep;
that voice made me want to draw near.

I got close and warmed in the light.
He smiled and welcomed completely.
Gratitude began to grow within.
Little did I know, He cleaned me.

That voice, like a match to my center,
ignited a fire at my hearth.
Walking away after conversation,
I kept His light to find life beyond earth.

I plumbed the depth of my heart
in a moment's despair, and with anger.
What a complete fail!
All I found were grudges and danger.

My process, less appealing each moment.
Giving in to exhaustion after waste.
Instructed by nature to rest.
In the midst of sorrow's abyss, I laid.

Sleep, a gifted, generous physician,
even after slowly tucking away,
goes right to work emptying and carrying.
In correction, sleep never delays.

Every necessary metabolic change
can be moved along once we dream.
Our body unlocks precious dynamics
after reading our precious buried stream.

On waking, my head oiled to shine.
Thoughts realign and I see,
Jesus plumbed the depths of my heart.
That Master, blessed withdrawal, perfect key.

No effort can erase that moment.
Absurd to my very fiber and element.
It was a divisive turn, completely aware
of internal separations, efforts spent.

Total comprehension shatters
the protection mode, now obvious.
Shame, a crushing jolt
as the mind decides "serious."

Regret, a deep ash burn
that left hidden, can forever smolder.
Christ looked at me and motioned
my weighty package to His shoulder.

Meditate on what I heard
as waking, I interrupted
all thought-provoking memory
meant for insertion and corruption.

My effort fails. My tear's salt burns.
Today, I handed feelings and impressions
to this Master who has studied me.
Let God insert gains, resist regression.

His effort sails all oceans;
it lifts all mountains.
He is the curtain of all skies,
and the source of holy fountains.

They said, "true thing", then they lied.
I wanted the treasure as its glitter impressed.
Such uncertainty about the truth brings lessons.
Opening their package, an empty quest.

Within was a very small package,
though its image seemed quite grand.
It had all the right colors and appeal.
It wore the mark of "best brand."

That first taste of so slim a purchase
both drew me, while disappointing.
Its promise, like an echo with volume.
Yet, its appeal was speedily going.

The tiny matter, traded for a vast treasure,
lacking ability to console, while distracting.
Quickly, that mistake, so clearly understood.
This whole belief, quite lacking.

The choice, so obviously wise to refund.
That lie, once treasured; better forgotten.
Replace those falsehoods with absolute.
Reduce time spent sobbing.

Hold out for the Truth. He will come
as you ask only softly, deep within.
He is so ready to deal well with us.
He has adopted us fully despite sin.

He responds completely to your interest.
His plan for you increases as you reach.
With His whole heart, He's lived to love.
With His whole life, we are His to teach.

With a shock, catapulted from a dream;
alert suddenly, while deep in a cave,
a kind friend knelt beside me.
He said, "Pilgrim, I've come here to save."

Unresponsive, yet, heard deep within,
my eyes opened slowly, so wet.
In that dream, alone, I'd been grieving.
I never knew any savior, not yet.

His warm hand on my shoulder reminded
me of Mother, of Father's hold on good.
With those two, so much nurturing,
but I knew everything, all I could.

I shook off those hands long ago
and ran headlong into the day.
I spent freely, burning every candle.
Up the glass, light the torch, ignore decay.

A foundation brought within me
began to dissolve under this condition,
and getting to stars in my head
became less possible, with zero fruition.

I'd looked down at myself after spending
at party after party, after waste.
Then fell into the cave, filthy,
comatose, forgetting about grace.

But that hand warmed my shoulder,
calling a sorrowful wretch from the grime
of the shattered ego, of knowing
everything wrong in your mind.

His warm smile and compassionate eyes,
told me, "Safe. Saved for claiming."
I gave up holding that spiritual blanket,
false, and filthy, that alone I had made me.

Drawn to stand up beside Him;
acceptance in His face, not disgust.
Forgiveness, a familial longing,
He has adopted this creation of dust.

Instead of plowing down to grind dust,
I chose today to take His hand.
Across dusted roads and life, I know
He leads to the Promised Land.

I knew you were beautiful
under all that decay.
I knew you before time.
You're the child that I made.

I imagined you
and fell directly in love.
You, my child, that spark!
You, my little cub.

As you walk your experience,
your feet collect clay.
As your Father, declared,
dirt must be washed away.

As I hold you close,
my desire to restore
from the mire of sin,
by the suffering I bore.

I bring you this water
to wash, to make holy.
As your Father, attended,
low, yet not lowly.

What remains humble is wise.
What is refreshed will rise.
When Christ washes our feet
we become His children and light.

That muck He removes
tried to color us "theirs",
but washed by our Father
we become His true heir.

The sun knew a change had come.
It perched far to the east, anxious.
Aware all had changed about day.
Totally braced, yet beaming and curious.

It rolled forward to shine peeking at earth.
Those rays sought out movement early.
It watched tender hearted disciples seeking
a body to grieve, yet oiled and precious, surely.

They arrived at the tomb, a small cave,
freshly dug and sealed firmly.
Of caves, this body had known intimate.
Born in one, now buried and murky.

But the rock! The mouth stood open.
No body to find, but a folded linen.
With heaven's news, an angel stood to greet them.
Heralded, truth of what was no longer hidden.

"Remember," the angel reminded,
all those revelations of future ahead.
"He said He would be raised in three days!"
He had spoken of a future beyond death!

The sun watched, already knowing
a great dawn had arrived hours earlier.
As its herald, beside angels, so excited,
it burned, joyful, as God's courier.

Gardens shook in joyful expression
as a Stranger affected them by presence.
A hooded being, unrecognized, our One.
A stave of wheat, a cup of wine, our tench.

"Are you the gardener?" Mary tearfully asked.
He stood and looked with such warmth,
this Man, alive, smiling and comforting.
She then saw Him clearly, divine form.

When I woke to see the scattered sky,
with sadness at yesterday's loss of life,
that same sun beamed upon the garden.
Rose blooms reminded as I cried.

That sun knew future holdings and homestead
had come, established, completed,
by every action, fulfilled prophecy, and miracles.
Death, now, but a whisper, wholly defeated.

Remember, the ladies went early,
spirits torn, to grieve before holy sod.
Instead, they found our Peace of Forever,
heaven on earth, in a Man Divine, the Toft!

The Roman soldiers marched
through dusty Jerusalem streets.
They brought uncertain care
to all their eyes should meet.

But those eyes reflected belief.
Their eyes had actually seen
the true Savior of what counts,
that rod of Aaron's, green.

Yet, human fear existed
as often neighbors hung to rot.
And suspicion, even hunting us
was the Roman, Saul's favorite lot.

But God blessed; we met in secret.
We memorized the Psalms.
We starved, but shared and lived.
We resisted earthly wants.

There was plague and filth,
common Roman destruction.
Still, we collected to whisper
true loving supplication.

The love of Bread could not be altered.
Adoration of the protective Door.
The candle burned in Greece.
That candle went north.

Burning across Asia,
forever facing threat
of governmental judgement,
of suffrage, of death.

It was carried across oceans.
It lived in holy sand.
God has blessed and allowed
testing through every land.

He asked us to seek only heaven.
From there a perfect answer will come.
As I hold on to certainty in only Him,
my constant prayer,
that Door welcomes me home.

The Plight of Sentinel Time

All time stands watch, recording.
Few human lives sonder equally.
Most eyes capture a snapshot.
Without true record, understood feebly.

Hindsight of the strong strike sharp.
Putting together such a puzzle,
and logically arriving at dawn,
strident hearts bare the pain, double.

Humans ravel and unravel constantly.
Construction of "anything," maybe good?
Yet, a mistake according to heaven.
Do His children do all they should?

In a creative space, across the Master's desk,
good are blessed, yet pricked by evil,
in a proving opportunity to identify
what is false, of lies, or the believable.

Those who watch, understanding clearly
what Princess Kassandra warned a thousand times,

Little king draws the nectar.
Flower loves to provide.

Patterns generous and destined to follow
the original design, so wise.

He carries the gold after lunch
to the family of brothers and wife.
His mind and purpose, only simple;
his efforts, his farm's source of life.

Our blessing, this hungry bee
makes more gold than he needs.
Our palates thank him, every drop
making buttery biscuits so sweet!

As the tree grew tall
and budded spring flowers,
as the fruit produced
fell from wind-blown bowers.

Tiny trees take root
and grow up tall to shine.
As the youths develop,
they are gathering at the rind.

This energy takes root,
surrounds their life as much evolves.
Encouragement to lean right
as elder's ideas cascade and fall.

Angels invited stand close
to the aged and the young.
They hover protectively fighting
the demonic throng.

We elder forest must guide
our tiny trees to focus on Jesus.
Nailed to a tree for our salvation,
and no matter how He sees us,

He watches our actions close,
as reflected, do we think like Him?
But He tries to fill our hearts,
and displace every bit of sin.

He said, "Bring the children."
Parents do as angels bless.
Parents prayerfully seek Him,
and those angels do their best.

Forever was the whole point at the start.
God, Jesus, and the Holy Spirit spun.
They were joyful and absolute family,
but God's plan to increase all won.

To bring home a family full of joy,
to bring a heavenly living room, His throne,
to span all creative, a shop, a universe,
to arrange a perfect heavenly home.

That family, a barrel of perfect apples.
His eye, that barrel, does the impossible.
God wants forever to be our place.
But extreme corrections, first probable.

Ready with sleeves rolled up and gloves
in His orchard, grafting arbor with care.
Then that perfect arborist watches,
guiding every bloom to its end to be paired.

Those apples that fall early to worm and rot.
The Gardener understands loss and gain.
He planted forever in that orchard.
Every apple kept for that grove is His aim.

I picked you up with all my strength.
I never knew I was that strong.
Perhaps, because how I love you,
and how we sang those songs.

You were broken and bleeding.
You even bled on my shoulder.
As a little brother that I treasure,
I could carry you like no other.

When the word came in, rescued,
I cried huge tears of gratitude.
Because, buddy, this life would be empty
without you, and that is the truth.

You were never heavy or unkind.
I don't know how I succeeded.
But brother, you're hanging in there.
Together for life, even bleeding.

Tearing off the smallest piece
of my heart to share with you
on a stormy afternoon, when found,
I saw that you felt blue.

My heart so brimming full of meaning;
giving some seemed natural.
Replacement comes by faith alone;
regrowth, only gradual.

My given piece, the gum
to paste together needed bandages;
my given piece to make a shield
to save you from the ravages.

Impulse within to offer free
this loving, trusting gift,
is just the kind of action, expanding,
that gives a needed lift.

As I lift you, as we hold hands,
together we discover,
the light, the good, this warm design
is credit of what hovers.

Our glow that grows can not
be seen by less than godly eyes.
And knowing what we felt was real,
nourishing, true, and right.

You reached me like the wind;
naturally blew into my yard.
I saw a beauty, but missed the rest,
and so, adopted you deep in my heart.

I could not predict how that sky drew you away.
It left me so hurt, profuse bleeding.
The river of salty tears could fill basins.
My only escape was fitful dreaming.

Your wings drew you far and wide,
and soft air currents delivered you.
Though you were so happy,
I just could not be soothed.

New winds blow, but I just smile.
I spent my fortune on your gale.
But I gave my heart to the Prince of Peace.
He pulled me from that hell.

Hell on earth, as humans fail,
but Jesus is quietly steady.
Pursuit of shredded, repairable souls,
His holy peace makes them ready.

What is a family?
You look like a brother.
And that elder woman I know
feels a bit like a mother.

In searching myself,
is there a sister inside?
Do I share what is bounty
or only offer blight?

Am I blighted, living without
holy rain, sunshine, and Word?
Do I seek others to help,
or on my throne, put myself first?

Am I the only lamp at my table?
Do I gain Him by respecting?
Am I the only value on earth?
Is there need seen, but neglecting?

Pulling up covers and not toss;
rise up to push instead.
Even Jesus showed us
His truth by raising the dead.

Instead of waiting for luck,
in lieu of projecting self-worth,
rely instead on doing,
and producing by effort first.

Smash the mirror and look
into faces, a reflection of me.
Christ has already provided
everything I need.

"Me, me, me! No!"
A very lonely team,
when surrounded by united hearts
is the more satisfying dream.

That answer, easy to read,
but first pick up the book.
Education about family
will reward you when you look.

What is a family?
It's preference for the best,
above my petty, and image,
above earthly crowns and crests.

Only one word is vital.
One word will persist forever.
That word, "love", as shown by God,
I know now; separate never.

We can just sit while our life ebbs,
meant to last a day at a time.
Thankful from my core at days
with sunshine, joy, and rhyme.

Each day, open space,
revealed only by minute,
and every single second
comes with a distinct limit.

Careful with ambition
as the sun tucks day away.
Gather all the good seeds.
Enjoy the remembrance of each day.

Beauty and beings of light inspires
my heart to respond as an angel.
Every flower enfolded, collected by me
is in abandon, tossed in the tangle.

My heart has collected precious lights,
such aromatic rose recollections.
Those dear treasured loves with no vessel,
as they tucked away, earth's reflection.

My angelic heart orders and straightens
every sorrow, tangle, and crease.
It stands absolute, as the lights hover,
that I will join you in heaven. You'll see.

I wasn't fishing, but you handed me dinner.
My rented heart, crying, yet you came.
That moment in kindness that you handed
to me, your best; it was not the same.

Left so long by the water, so hungry.
Barnacles of sorrow scored my back.
But your power arrived just then,
and shattered spirit, restored, intact.

It was your smile, glowing, so gentle.
It was the wind of you, lifting and repairing,
because you're living spirit, such nutrition.
Of other's neglect, just no comparing.

I thank God, He found good and sent her.
I recall the sharp darkness and tears.
Yet, today, as I dine beside the benefactor,
God has shown me rescue from fears.

God has shown me His finest precious daughter.
I've been befriended by heaven and you.
This lift from scouring, so undeserved.
It's your unmercenary kindness. God knew.

We stood together in the roses.
Your Fathering hug, my needed gesture.
These days have been grinding,
and every value seems false measure.

This heart connects completely to thought,
and knowing by education has taught.
Logical arguments shred oily
the informed, the reports, and the lot.

Yet, this morning a sun rose undaunted.
The garden could not withhold its bloom.
Running from the shadows of my worry,
running to be blessed by prayerful food.

Arriving so sudden at the very center,
I spin around, inhale, and seek you.
Your essence, always accompanied,
so generous to rescue this fool.

Your first blessing warms my face.
The roses lift and prepare
my heart for such in-rushing blessings.
You've planted roses along heaven's stairs.

Remember when it felt so good,
your good day, a foregone known.
You stepped out into the rose garden
and smelled the blooming rose.

Its dusty place occupied
by that certainty and wonderment,
sometimes seems so missing
or just up and left.

Never let go of that brilliant sight.
Be in charge and tell Worry, "No."
Dust off what must be cleaned.
Repair what needs to be sewn.

There blooms a rose garden
within your sunshine heart.
In rising, the truth is,
that's the place to start.

The sun had found a tree bow bending.
It shined through leaves as if lace.
Specs of gold arrived below
falling with natural grace.

The sky on the other side was jealous.
It could not see through the branch.
Sweet pink and blue erupted
as flowers, joyful, seemed to dance.

Scenes of beauty, view of calm.
The wild near us always calls,
and begs our eyes to drink up.
No one on earth can capture all.

When that sun dapples the trail,
as the melodious wind blows soft,
open up and look about.

It's a great day to take a walk.

While on the journey, along the way,
we met briefly and joined hands.
My eyes looked out past your shoulders
as behind you, spread scenic lands.

We drew a breath of morning air,
then exhaled life spent, well used.
I was so grateful to my maker
for sending me you, my muse.

I hold that foggy moment in
a softened hallway within.
When I miss you, heart yearning,
I can go sit there, dear friend.

There will never be that moment.
I can't fathom a time ever,
when without reflex, I would erase
one sweet second of you, never.

The weather had good provision
for that chosen cherry tree.
This spring, nature's kindest moment
came as wind ruffled it freely.

And that tree stood as a sentry
at the highest edge of cliff,
examining its valley.
Not one detail was missed.

Then that morning the mountain woke.
It shook and rumbled, then expelled
its lava, pouring across the ground,
and its level waxed and swelled.

As the blooming cherry tree
expressed tender pink delights.
That lava burned its path
creating a most exciting sight.

That living tongue of flaming red
ran past the crested roots.
Such sated passion excites us,
but the tree, blessed by pale rosy hues.

After peace there will be red.
The field is full and bloomed.
Gather them by the bunch;
jar and water them to fight gloom.

Red sparkles and strikes
like a flame flickers, like an ax.
It reminds of luck and heartbeats.
It coats and declares with no slack.

These red valleys, awake during peace.
They recall sad past days, meditation.
They announce heroic pasts of stories!
Bloom after bloom, next generation.

Beauty is near in a petal, in the air.
At your feet is substance, yet dun.
At the nook, down the hill, runs a river.
Above, freely shining, is moon and sun.

We start with a quiet calming gauze.
Dirt, black to brown, full of rot.
Yet, what erupts and provides,
given touch, can be quite a lot!

Begin self, this moment, with thanks.
Simple, in giving, all thought and act.
Accountants unaccounted work every hour.
They record perfectly, the unvarnished facts.

Translated now or at its God chosen moment.
Presenting before you or to others unknown,
God translates perfectly what He values.
For His mercy, His loved ones seek to atone.

Inhale deeply of holy. You are the garden.
Go outside, breath and collect sunshine.
Trust is something you must practice.
Precious apples! Be grafted to the vine!

Grace showers down as we live,
laughing, aspiring, learning, and growth.
We pray for roses and sunny days,
but in the end get what is sown.

Pick your thoughts like planning the garden.
Give up hate, destructive.
Become that grace, your earthly efforts
can be the source of construction.

Our appellations are heard on high.
The angels carry and deliver.
With bounty so lovely, crisp, contenting,
summer, mother, and grace given.

Patterns

God knew what He was doing, exactly,
as He sat at work designing life.
Every relevant detail included
as He whistled a future hymn and smiled.

Growing from beginnings He produced,
spiraling into time that had no clock,
lining up each woven end to perfection.
His sacred presence, energy that never stops.

The leaf lives on in admiration of His decision.
It receives its blessings, silently grateful.
I woke up to understand this
and to live in His grace, forever thankful.

The hill stood stalwart, patient.
A somber rain drifted, lazy.
Every tree on that hill
was waking seasonal, yet hazy.

The ice and snow had melted,
The trees, bare, felt spring's contact.
Of inner activity for expanding
from the heart, bled no lack.

Branches, dreaming of summer,
reached farther seeking range.
They could calculate distance.
They instinctively understand space.

No danger can bring them fear.
Time can only dress and undress.
Standing within a crowd of trees,
beside friends, dispelling stress.

As my company, they are loyal.
As my neighbor, they only guard.
When the summer breezes blow
their branches whisper through the yard.

The Sweet Annie blooms, hearty,
and apple blossoms perfume,
but so soon autumn howls.
In the dream we'll call back June.

That summer night by the bay,
that silver moon beamed bright.
It seemed more a dark afternoon,
cooled by mystique and dight.

Quivering in anticipation; memories.
Flying almost, yet toes don't reach.
No earlier disappointment could hinder
the aching yearning to just sing.

Climbing firm into the swing before
a precipice and rocky waves below,
I believe, anyway, in such miracles as flight.
There is no fall, only rise into the glow.

Every time, such a smile, so deep my joy.
This time counted precious; now, the flower.
It's in the levitating joy each time.
That pen, those words, prose' power.

The tree got very excited.
It felt crispness in the air.
It felt that cloud-heaviness.
It stretched those branches, bare.

A little tinkling sound of bells,
a magical moment delight,
then clouds let go the cottony tufts
to cling to a world of night.

As the fluffy white display
tried to pillow to the ground,
those branches received the overflow
and branch tips soon to round.

Bells tinkle in memory of the arbor
holding loose to winter dander.
Snow softly fluffed and blown,
or whispers at the landing.

There was water in the air
as the round moon rose to glow
over night's melodic beauty.
It became a mist rainbow.

The birds all tucked away,
Rodents scampered, curious.
Crickets played their harped legs,
and beetles buzzed hard, but spurious.

All the glow blessed the forest.
The rainbow of mist, a cellophane,
and the occasional punctuating hoot
of a bird ready to hunt game.

I stood at the dusty street's edge.
The sky looked down, less distressed.
Many neighbors had lately been worried.
Media said all was a mess.

I looked at the eyes needing sleep.
We waited for our late conveyance.
I saw scowls and sensed such want.
How could nothing make sense?

After praying, the moment I woke,
calmed, my heart understood.
Peace, my fuel and pair of glasses,
I will put first, before want, only good.

Looking at the parting cloud above,
rising by heartfulness from the dust,
the wagon at end to collect me
will be driven only by the just.

The world is like God's first bank.
It's full of dander, dust, and value.
He knows what every crumb is worth.
He will pay every penny due.

His goal, to ransom a precious Son
to buy the entry for all intended,
and in great glory, Son restored,
pain and all sadness comes to ending.

In the midst of all His gold
He placed a brick upon the ledge.
Inside that clay fortress, His family.
To be a tree like Jesus, not a sedge.

To bare the gold like His leaves,
to be a witness for His church,
to be surrounded by His love,
to spread the gold of His true words.

What a strange and wonderful feeling,
to discover you were important and wise,
to the heart and purpose of another,
and discovered this completely by surprise.

It's a knowing devoid of ego,
that secret understanding held aloft,
just beyond your knowledge,
protected and held in hearted halls.

Such a dynamo strike to my image,
the one that I scold in reflection.
There is nothing more healing and kind
than the most precious reflective affection.

I saw a bevy of clouds.
They were lofty and gorgeous.
There were great beams of light
cast as though I were important.

Tears filled my eyes
as I thought of your discord,
and yet, having you, my friend,
my whole being, favored.

Be soothed where you are,
surrounded by these rays.
God's light can always find
those friends for whom we pray.

Not perceptible to the eyes,
but to your very core.
Beyond the rays, God waits.
He is simply holding the door.

His patience, always perfect,
as we spend every minute given.
Soon, but not too soon,
together, we'll skip into heaven.

A dream ascended full of mystery, yet light.
It rose from murk of all stored memory.
Its message to my conscience for unraveling, alert,
and accompanied by every sensory.

Crusty dreams salt the corner of my eyes.
My hand easily brushes them away.
Yet, a heavy message spoken, dreamy
calls my mind and opinions, "Please stay."

The awakening considers landscapes, raw.
Existing, yes, here in my garden.
All those dreamy friends, our glasses raised,
the dearly beloved and the ardent.

In the multifaceted land, my lot,
all I see, and what was given,
are blessed loaves of bread, sustaining
how those dream's reflections lead to heaven.

Love me as I am, raw, spiritually alive!
Forget me if what is here was too much.
As we forget those silly human measurements,
our hearts discover, God made no such.

There is always Hope, and we are family.
Come into my song, see how I'm united
by all the singing I ever heard.
Under heaven, all that I dream, righted.

What I gave at the start
was shallow and common.
The gift of heaven, so amazing,
 but given to this onion.

We peeled one layer,
a small admission,
and more of self-soothing.
A whole lot less listen.

Some mercy, a seed took hold.
Soon another, and a garden grew.
Rapidly peeling my onion,
revealing every sinful clue.

So many rainbows and blessings.
Constant garden companion.
Rainstorms, floods, and losses.
Rake out debris; peel your onion.

As the onion is examined
layer by layer, the pelf torn loose.
Deeper, tossing finished to rot.
Garden provides shade and food.

Till that onion is peeled to its core,
till my last step alive on this earth,
gardening prayerfully beside the Gardener,
seeking miracles, not gold or dirt.

I was in my heart, regretting.
A heart stabbed a million times.
But as I hummed a soothing tune,
I saw most cuts were from inside.

He told us His flesh was bread.
He confessed He is the door.
He's the vine, the wine, the leaf!
Parables explain facts, not lore.

Yet, after all He has promised,
and all He revealed,
doubt nibbles when faced with shadow.
Nothing will remain concealed!

Just like that, that shadow rose
and loomed menacingly, yet weak.
But His word carved by His finger
inside me stomps it by Wheat.

Strength of spirit recedes
as we transfixed on deep wounds.
But like a rod I know, in Aaron's hand,
that Word emboldens and blooms.

Crushed by His candle, a tiny whisper,
the giant shadow, forgotten, unknown.
As my rising from low for His adoption
causes my whole future to glow!

He asked, "Do you want to be healed?"
It was a direct question.
He said, " Blessed is he that lights
the candle." Parabolic lessons!!!

Words increase in meaning as we study,
within the walls of our own hearts.
We should have learned first from Jesus.
That's exactly where He starts.

Mother chickadee landed stealthy.
She called her tiny fledge.
In her beak she held breakfast,
a worm found on a sedge.

Yet, her eyes spied a small cotton ball
attached beneath the branch.
She perceived far more nutrition,
thankful to catch this by chance.

That cotton ball began to open.
Little black dessert rushed forth.
Her fledgling, so pampered by spiders,
the day the baby spiders got born.

That storm exploded outside.
No one expected a twister.
The ominous dark clouds bore down.
Where its tip road the ground was a fissure.

It kept moving directly toward the house.
It dragged an angry, destructive tail.
The wind was furiously ripping at tiles.
Its profound presence, a moaning wail.

On my knees, with a plaintive request,
in the living room, watching it aim.
When all they find is splinters,
it will be nature's force to be blamed.

Yet, just before certain destruction,
with a tremulous turning, uncertain,
that twister decided another direction,
and all misery or details unlearned.

When do we know it's all over?
At what point do we decide for God?
At that moment of true ending, and not before.
Live fiercely; no rush to that sod.

Decided, that end, already written.
You are the co-author by self-direction.
There is always infinitely possible,
natural movement that brings correction.

Warnings, exciting misses, off-days,
all will come, some misses, some strikes.
No matter every outcome,
not foregoing one second of life.

Dark shadows will always be dark.
Illness will always be in the margin.
But fear is not worth one penny spent.
Faith till all departures is my target.

They knew me by the coat,
not the hidden truth of my life.
I would not interrupt their musings
although, stained and dyed, that coat was a lie.

I did not withhold that fact at confession.
My feet trotted forward quietly admitting.
My cross I felt, unseen by others.
My foot soles hiding sinning.

Jesus came up beside me.
I felt the cross grow lighter.
He said, "Let me guide you
and you will live much wiser."

Still, not sharing my closeted
work with the world,
I continue each day
with a pattern of Sure.

Letting Him share my journey's efforts
took time to reveal truth of faith.
As He loved and held me,
loneliness, complete fade.

Success becomes morning prayers,
holding dear time spent with Him.
You find as love grows trust,
you've changed a lot within.

Plod along; that coat will be replaced.
Your mind refreshed; calm on your face.
To join Him now and later;
no better way.

My heart was once so very protected,
polished, and stroked for the glow.
But a soft spot occurred somehow,
and inside, that patch began to grow.

Oh, what pain, it's crusty cover
cracking apart and revealing meat.
Tears oozing out and ache setting in.
My soul cried out, "Just go to sleep!"

Instead, I held on through the day.
I smiled instead of shedding tears.
Christ smiled at me inside the cracks.
His look and lift erased fears.

With time, the bearing showed gain.
No one but God truly knows.
His hands, our surgeon, sews with grace.
Later, this greatness will glow.

Christ spoke to my grieving heart
in a gentle, silent impression.
He said tears are safe, as approaching,
He walked across that sea, blessing.

From lowly, reaching, I took His hand,
and He pulled me from oceans I'd cried.
He held me, rocking His little lamb,
then set me down to dry.

Lessons repeat as I climb toward land.
That promise defeats day's new fear.
But for Jesus, though always with you,
to reach, you have to want to be near.

Rescued from selfish ends by choice,
His effort deeply calms.
That steady hand above the water,
His beautiful songs and Psalms.

Whether smiles come your way,
whether your friends say good-bye,
whether your health hits a road,
whether your heart knows only cry,

This profound light existed
before we even came to be.
Love brought Him to make us,
so forever with Him we'll be.

Look through those tearful eyes
into this Lover of Man's face.
As you do, joy will find you
and surround you with His Grace.

When you're getting close to God,
Satan knows and starts to cry.
With all his silly little might, against you,
prickles start to fly.

So when you're stabbed in the back,
when you're pulled down to be trod,
remember who you gave your heart to,
the most insightful, awesome God.

He will hold you as you bleed
and record your every tear.
He's the one who plans to keep you,
correcting wrong, and hold you dear.

He will protect you from that worm.
You are beautiful, His garden rose.
He is clearing acres and building mansions
for those loved ones that He chose.

The palate of God, the palm of a hand,
the splash of the sky, the mirror of sea.
In my eyes God's love always reaches
to bestow heaven with thee.

All that is wonder, and all that is good
will continue, be healed, and the blessing.
From fertilizer comes life.
Soon, comes the redressing.

We lay on His desk and He works.
This beauty, not the finished masterpiece,
and I intend to forever farm there.
To that end, He builds my future lease.

His gentle hand turns the child beloved.
His effect, growth, intelligent choosing.
As He prays for His dear lot,
not one heart belonging is ever losing.

CPSIA information can be obtained
at www.ICGtesting.com
Printed in the USA
BVHW040919070122
625371BV00026B/1349

9 781638 372950